Falling Mangoes

Being aware of every moment

Amanda Ruberto

Dedications

For my mom, who has always been my main support system and has encouraged me to be my most authentic self even though at times she didn't understand my spontaneous life choices. She loves me more than wildflowers love fresh air.

For V. Vajiramehdi, who believed in my ability to be a great spiritual teacher the moment he met me. I will be forever grateful to him for taking me under his wing to share his wisdom of the Buddha's teachings, and for all of the kindness and compassion he had for me. He invited me to Rai Cherntawan International Meditation Center in Chiang Rai, Thailand, which he founded, and I lived there for two months, learning more about meditation. I want to thank him for giving me such a great opportunity to teach yoga there as well prior to doing the twenty-six-day Vipassana course at another center.

For my friend Jason, who was like a brother to me and is no longer here with us. Every time I sweep now, I think of him, and as tears tend to trickle down during those moments, I remind myself of the peace he noticed in me while I was sweeping in our home last summer in Venice Beach, California. To which he said, "Did you sweep in Thailand or something?" And I responded, "Yes, actually I did, every day for twenty-six days when I was meditating in a monastery!"

Lastly, for my grandad, who inspired me to travel the world ever since I was a little girl. Every time I went to visit him, he'd pull out big picture albums of his worldwide travel adventures, telling me stories and teaching me about different cultures and religions. When I was eight years old, he showed me pictures of monks in Thailand, and I was forever intrigued. I was amazed to hear that some of these monks who wore robes were living in silence and with a mission of attaining inner peace. It was during my last cup of tea with him in early October 2017 in Toronto, where I brought over a photo album I made and showed him pictures from my travels. As we flipped through the pages I said, "And this is when I did a twenty-six-day silent meditation course. Oh, and this was the temple that I practiced in every day in Chiang Mai." To which his response was, "Well, you find out things about yourself that you never realized." And he was right. I learned so much about myself during moments of stillness and complete surrender.

I didn't know at the time this would be my last cup of tea with him, as he sadly passed away later that month. He kept telling me I need to write a book. So here it is, Grandad, this one is for you. Enjoy reading it in heaven.

XoXo ♥

Preface

Falling Mangoes is a personal journal of what it is like journeying through the art of meditation. When seeking inner peace, there is only one way to look: within. This is exactly what I did.

Meditating on average ten to twelve hours a day, I bring you through my experience of living in a Thai monastery with monks among other international and local meditators. It hits every emotional button and brings humor to situations I am left to deal with. When I wrote my age on the registration form—twenty-six—I took it as a sign I was meant to do the twenty-six-day meditation, when only intending to do ten. With perseverance and patience, I show a glimpse of what daily life was like and how the power of meditation can change your life through insight, love, compassion, forgiveness, gratitude, and inner peace.

If you can, I invite you to light a candle and some incense, play relaxing music, and brew a nice cup of tea. Find a comfortable place in your home, at your work, in a hammock, in nature, or wherever you may find yourself in this very moment. Now close your eyes and take a few deep breaths in and out while mindfully connecting to your heart. And as you gently open your eyes, please open your mind as I take you on a spiritual journey...

Introduction

Vipassana means to see things as they really are, to observe the body, its sensations and become aware of any insights that might come about during mindful meditation.

We are now in Chiang Mai, Thailand. We have passed the main gates of the Wat Rampoeng Meditation Center to begin a twenty-six-day meditation course. Before we begin, let me share the eight precepts that must be obeyed. By giving up these things, even just temporarily, helps us to recognize and reduce our attachments. By spending time without these things, we have the opportunity to focus on practicing meditation and experiencing a happiness not based on material things.

The Eight Precepts:

1. Abstaining from killing.
2. Abstaining from stealing.
3. Abstaining from sexual activity.
4. Abstaining from telling lies.
5. Abstaining from intoxicating drinks and drugs.
6. Abstaining from eating in the afternoon.
7. Abstaining from entertainment and beautifying the body.
8. Abstaining from using luxurious furniture.

Here is your daily routine while you are here:

4 a.m. – The bell or your alarm clock wakes you up for practice. Starting with mindfulness, you will practice walking, then sitting meditation.

*Always start with "mindful walking" then when you stop walking, take your place immediately for the sitting practice.

6 a.m. – The bell rings for breakfast. It is your responsibility to follow the bell and arrive in the dining hall on time, because prayers are chanted before each meal. Latecomers will not be served. Alms food is considered sacred; take only as much as you will eat. Eat slowly, mindfully, and preferably alone. This means no talking—do not make conversation during or after meals, as doing so is disruptive to mindfulness. Wash your dishes immediately after eating. Taking care of your rubbish; there is a place for it near the sink where you wash your dishes. Then, it is again time for practice until the bell rings for lunch.

10:30am – The bell rings for lunch. Follow the same guidelines as breakfast.

12pm – Continue your meditation practice.

3pm – Time for reporting with the monks and then continue your meditation practicing until evening time.

*Reporting is done on a daily basis to check in with the monks to report how many hours you've done for the day and how you are doing with your overall practice. They will advise you on the meditation techniques in which you will be learning and practicing as well as give answers to any questions or problems you may want to inquire about.

10pm – Sleeping may begin, while dressed in your white clothing.

~

All right, now that we got the rules and schedule, LET'S DO THIS!

Monday, June 1, 2015

The Update

First things first: Facebook update! Friends and family need to know I'll be "off the grid." Don't want to cause a panic by all of a sudden going MIA while traveling in Asia solo.

"Gone meditating at the most hardcore meditation center in Southeast Asia! While registering for a ten-day Vipassana retreat today in Chiang Mai, I was told there's an option for ten or twenty-six days as well. So when I wrote my age down on the form, twenty-six, I thought why not spend a day meditating representing each year of my life? I can reflect and show myself how grateful I am for all of these years of living. This will be extremely difficult, and when I'm having a hard day, I will think of the challenges I had gone through at the age of what day I am at. I believe this will give me the strength and courage I need to keep going. Some of the rules I will follow are wake up every day at 4 a.m., no talking to anyone, no using the internet or phone, no listening music or reading, must wear white at all times, and cannot eat past noon. I will be meditating for over ten hours a day and basically just be in my own world. They say the benefits of self-transformation are profound. I am ready and know I can do it! Please send me love and good vibes. I'll need it.

Like I always say "Go big or go home!."

Special comments I received:

Gabrielle: I'm very excited for this journey for you darling flower!!! It will be the most transforming and light filled gift! See you on the other side beautiful one....

Sarah: This is amazing! Good luck love! I can't wait to talk with you after about it!! xo

Emerson: Proud of you!

Brandie: Wow. Incredible Amanda. Your path inspires mine!!

Gayle: Sounds amazing. If it's allowed, keep a journal of your experiences. Love and light x

If it wasn't for the above comment, this book wouldn't even exist.

So, THANK YOU for inspiring the idea of keeping a journal. I was not supposed to do any writing during the course, but I made a special request prior to starting, asking the head monk for foreign meditators if I could document my experience. He gave the okay.

Mom: Sending Love Amanda!

Momo: That is huge darling – 10 days are hard enough! Good luck!

Emily: SO amazing. I will send you mind messages each night instead of Skype. Technology is so overrated anyway x

Kyla: That's amazing, Amanda! You can totally do it. Lots of love and positive energy to you! Xo

France: In my meditation every day I will send you much love and good vibes.

Papa: Wow Bella Very Impressive!

Rika: Love ya Berto

Heather: I'm SO proud of you Amanda! You are incredible and you will come out of this shining brighter than ever before! I love you.

Tymara: Sounds amazing Amanda! I can't wait to hear all about it!

Brittney: I got goosebumps just reading this. U are amazing. Ready. Set. Transform beautiful baby. Blessings and deep breaths to you.

Ashara Love: Holding you in the light!

Liza: You can totally do it and get so much out of it. Going within is such a beautiful journey.

Santhat: Awesome!

Salvatore: Excellent decision. But is a bit long period if you're not real strong. My best wish. Ciao

Krukid: Very good.

Julio: Good energy is been sent...

Valerie: Amazing!

Sutiruck: Very good.

Tuesday, June 2, 2015

Day 1 Vipassana

10:15 p.m. – There's a cockroach in my sink. I went to wash my face, and when I turned on the tap, it ran out, scared the daylights out of me. Now it is hiding in the little hole on the back of the sink, all I can see is one antenna. Ugh. I just want to get ready for bed. *Peace, peace, compassion, compassion.* I need to bring it outside. I have Kleenex ready to catch him. No luck, he's not coming out. I guess he's sleeping in there tonight. I'm going to keep the door closed so he doesn't come out when I'm sleeping.

I just put honey on my face. V. Vajiramehdi gave me a bottle and said to put it on my face at night for good skin. He is a Master monk whose meditation center is in Chiang Rai, called Rai Cherntawan, where I was living for two months prior to doing my twenty-six-day silent meditation retreat. I met him while I was traveling in Japan, and he invited me to teach yoga and meditation at his center in northern Thailand. I ended up flying there the following week, and it was the best decision of my life! Now, here I am. I left there to come here, as he went on an Australian teaching tour.

Meditation and facials, my kind of night! Except for the washroom situation. So the night Master was leaving, on the thirtieth, he asked me what my plan was. I said, "I want to do Vipassana." He recommended Wat Rampoeng Meditation Centre in Chiang Mai and said it is a very good place to learn. "You must practice, practice, practice in order to become really good at something. Learn about Dharma, then you can teach the world." He helped me look up the website, and not being able to load the page, he told me to call them. I asked the man who answered the phone when the next ten-day course is and he said June second. Perfect timing, I thought. I told Master I was going to do it. We got pictures together and said our good-byes. "Master, I'll miss you."

"Who are you? I forget about you, everything is impermanent." He said laughing.

"Don't you remember me? Amandy from Kyoto?"

"Kyoto? What is Kyoto?" We burst out laughing. Good times, never a dull moment.

The next morning I met a half-Thai, half-Italian monk, twenty years old. We chatted, and his mom overheard me say I was going to Chiang Mai.

"You want to go to Chiang Mai?"

"Yes."

"We are going today, you can catch the bus with us. Meet here at 12:30 p.m."

By the time I finished packing my bag, it was already 1 p.m. I got a ride to the bus at 2 p.m., and they were nowhere in sight. They must have already gone, I thought. The next bus was at 5:30 p.m., so I bought a ticket for that. I arrived to Chiang Mai at 8:30 p.m. With nowhere to sleep yet—I was supposed to sleep at the mom's friend's house who I met this morning, but I didn't have her number to get in touch. I felt calm and not worried. I walked around the bus station and noticed a monk who looked like the one I met earlier. No way! It was them! I felt so relieved. When you are meant to connect with people, you will. Turned out, they went to a different bus station in Chiang Rai. So I got a ride with them and dropped the son off at a temple, a Burmese one, so he could sleep there. And we went back to the moms friend's beautiful home where I slept for the night. Then the next day, we went back to the Burmese temple, and I prayed for Lord Buddha's birthday and met a woman who gave me a monk's number who lives at a meditation center in Yangon, Burma. We had lunch there and I did healing on a guy's foot that was swollen due to diabetes.

We went back to the friend's home to rest for the night and then woke up and had coffee on the side of the house where there were big koi fish and lotus flowers. The son who was practicing as a monk decided that he wanted to do the silent meditation course with me too! So we went and got him from the temple and headed to Wat Rampoeng to register.

Today I arrived at the center at 8 a.m. Put on my white outfit, *sabai* (white sash), and brought my stuff in my room. We first did walking meditation, then sitting meditation. I attended the opening ceremony, then did walking and sitting meditation on and off for fifteen minutes each until 10 p.m. It is a full moon tonight, such a good day to start this course. I am going to do twenty-six days! *So* hard-core. Going to purify each year of my life. I'm twenty-six years old now and focusing on self-development. The mind is where it begins. I hope to become my best self and transform into a beautiful butterfly. Let the meta-morphosis begin!

Shanti, shanti. Which means peace, peace in Sanskrit. Going to wash my face now then go to bed, I have to wake up at 4 a.m. And yes, I was a little hungry around 4 p.m. and when I got to my room after 10 p.m. But now I'm okay.

"I am a meditator. Doing, doing, doing," said the monk over and over. "No eye contact, no interruption."

Wednesday, June 3, 2015

Vipassana Real Day 1

So I guess yesterday did not count since on our forms they only wrote the hours from yesterday and today as Day 1 on the form. Today was a pretty easy day. The bell woke me up at 4 a.m. I got up, had a body shower, then went to the meditation hall. Did walking and sitting meditation on and off for two hours. The bell rang for breakfast at 6:30 a.m. The hall was completely full with meditators and monks. We started with chanting for about ten minutes, maybe longer. I was sitting with vegetarian noodles and a banana in front of me, just wanting to eat. I was so hungry.

After breakfast, I layed in my room for fifteen minutes (may have had a power nap). We're not allowed to sleep during the day. Then I swept my room and went back to the hall for the 8 a.m. session, where I did more meditation, then the bell rang at 11:30 a.m. for lunch. I liked lunch better because we had watermelon, papaya salad, and greens. Much more my style than noodle soup for breakfast. I washed my dish by hand, then went back to my room. Took fifteen minutes' rest and did some stretching (yoga). I went back to the hall at 12:30 p.m. and meditated until 5:30 p.m. I went for walks in between to get water and go for washroom breaks. It was seriously starting to feel like it would be a long time till bed.

I had my first report with the monk. I love his energy. I told him, "I felt total bliss this morning, got restless around 4 p.m., and anger came up once really strongly. Then I focused on my feet, and it disappeared." The past came up a lot. It was easier to observe and let it go than it used to be. I'm becoming aware of my thought patterns, and through meditation they will change, as I'll have more control.

"I also saw many images on the floor while doing walking meditation of faces and people. Then I'd stop and look at the whole image, and after, I'd try to find it again," I told him. He said this happens and to not get attached. It's a craving of wanting to see the image again. He said to just notice them and say, "seeing, seeing, seeing, thinking,

thinking, thinking." One of the images was of a monk meditating in the mountains; I felt like it was Dharamsala, the Dalai Lama's place of residence in northern India. Another was a pregnant angel; she had big angel wings.

Other faces came up too. This has been happening for a few days now. First, I saw a very obvious face on someone's phone screen. Then, in a photo I took of an advertising board in Chiang Mai that turned out blurry, I could see a few faces in it. When I turned the picture sideways, it looked like my most recent bedroom from Vancouver, Canada.

I put a honey mask on my face, then washed it off and put coconut oil all over my body and drank a table spoon of it. The coconut oil is so good for you! I want amazing-looking skin. I have to take care of myself now if I want good skin when I'm older.

Love you, Amanda.

Sweet dreams and good night XoXo ♥

Thursday, June 4, 2015

Vipassana Day 2

5:15 p.m. – The day I got here, I registered for the course and was shown my room. We walked past the room next to mine and I saw a lady standing inside as I looked through the screen door. To the right of the door hung a sign that read "Determination." It was a little intimidating, not going to lie. What did this mean? Determination is at the end of the twenty-six-day course when you meditate for three days straight with no sleep. I really had no interest in me of doing this.

Pretty hard-core and kind of freaky. The next day the sign was still on her door. You are not allowed to leave your room at all, and you are brought two bags of food daily. Yesterday I noticed the sign was gone and thought, *Wow, she did it.* I saw her this morning at breakfast and thought again, *Wow, she did it.* She looked bright.

I just finished sitting meditation for twenty-five minutes, then the bell rang. It's rung by a monk and is very loud. I came to my room, and as I passed the office I saw the same woman, short red hair, white clothes, about five nine. She had her blue backpack on and was ready to head out of here! "She's free!" I said to myself. I felt so excited for her. I got a flash as if that will be me one day. When my time is done here and my next adventure will begin. Twenty-six days, though, it's still pretty intimidating, even though I want to do it. A lot of commitment to a lot of practice.

Sitting, sitting, sitting, walking, walking, walking.

Today I felt restless, I'd open my eyes about ten minutes into sitting. Looking at the clock, looking at the stopwatch. Again and again. Tired from the heat and had a headache on and off. Well, the day's almost over. I just had some soy milk, and there's a cat on my bed. It walked in as I was writing this. I started saying, "Peace is every step" during my walking meditation. It's written as an art piece by at Rai Cherntawan International Meditation Center where I was living in Chiang Rai, and it finally makes sense to me. Also very helpful to walk peacefully. Tonight was difficult. I was restless in the last sitting, meditated three and a half hours straight. BED!

Friday, June 5, 2015

Vipassana Day 3

3 p.m. – I just came to my room to drink some milk. My fan is on full blast, and I'm still feeling tired. I've meditated for six and a half hours already today. When I went back after a water break, I could not get the patience to walk as slow as I could for twenty-five minutes. The first day we started with fifteen minutes walking and sitting, then twenty minutes the second day, and twenty minutes today. I have been meditating very well today, though. One time I walked only one line in twenty-five minutes, about 10 meters. My technique is to take three full breaths before each step. Sometimes I imagine Master walking in front of me outside on the hardwood patio and in the forest where all the trees line up at Rai Cherntawan. I hope he is very proud of me for doing this. It takes a lot of patience, hard work, and discipline.

On the first night when we started to practice, I was lowering my right hand onto my left hand on my lap. As I was sitting looking at my hand, it looked like it was dead and reminded me of a hand in a coffin. I then realized one day this would happen and I won't have my body anymore. My eyes began to water as I said, "I love my body, I love my body, I love my body." Feeling like I take it for granted sometimes made me feel so grateful for it, but at the same time I felt a deep sense of impermanence. It was an overwhelming feeling knowing I won't have my body forever, and I know I should love it as much as I can while I have it. I need to take care of my body. And right now, I need to develop my mind so that it becomes strong. My body will come next. First strong mind, then strong body.

When I get out of here, I am really going to focus on getting in shape—strong, toned, and fit. Much love to ya, girl! Time to go back and meditate. Do not think about how many days are left!!! Focus on today; one day at a time.

Saturday, June 6, 2015

Vipassana Day 4

"I don't need to be accepted by anyone, I just need to accept myself." A thought that just crossed my mind as I was drying my hair from the fan on my bedroom wall. I have been so self-conscious of the dark circles under my eyes since I was a young girl or teen. It's like I was cursed with black eyes. I didn't know why; I figured it was from lack of sleep as a child. I would never want to be seen with darkness. I covered it up with makeup, every single day. I would not leave my house without being covered. I would always have concealer with me. I would go to a washroom, no matter where I was, and put more concealer on to hide the dark circles. I got insecure just thinking about if other people noticed. I felt ugly and exhausted-looking if the circles weren't covered. I believe what triggered this is when I was around fourteen, someone asked me one time if I got punched in the eye. It made me feel so insecure. But really, when I think of it now, it's not that big of a deal and it's not that bad. Dark circles under people's eyes are so common, especially when lacking sleep, or it could also be a vitamin deficiency. Who knows.

Since wearing makeup is not permitted, today I am not going to wear any. I had only been applying a little bit of concealer up until today. I just showered and feel amazing. It doesn't matter what other people think of me. It matters how I feel about myself. I want to get over this insecurity and feel comfortable in my own skin. My eyes are the light, and there can't be light without darkness, right?

XoXo I love you, Amanda.

2 p.m. – I'm not perfect, but I am trying to follow the rules as best I can. Have to admit, I just woke up from a nap. I am so tired in the afternoons and I've been up since 4 a.m. My head is throbbing too. It must be the heat. Well, time for me to go meditate again. I'm really feeling ten days is good for me. I have to extend my visa, and I want to see more of Thailand! Ow, my head. Observing thoughts. Compassion, be gentle with myself. What I am doing isn't easy. Stay with it, Amanda. Be here now.

During my last sitting, I thought about having yoga and meditation retreats at my camp. Either a weekend or week. People could sleep in tents, and the food would be all vegetarian. I also thought about having a spirit festival where vendors could come and set up for healing, psychic readings, massage, tarot, et cetera. I would also invite local food vendors and have yoga and meditation classes! I could build a yoga studio!

I also thought about how I can travel the world for free. I would be an inspiration to people of all ages to let go of their thoughts that it is too expensive, or they would have to wait till they have more money. Money is a block that prevents many people to travel. Of course you do need money, but I want to prove you can do it without money and show that there are kind people everywhere. When you have a mission to help others and share your talents, abilities, and skills, traveling the world isn't as hard as it seems. Plus, there are many jobs available all over the world. And if you want to travel, I suggest getting out there, go to different countries, and new opportunities will show themselves to help you be able to live, eat, and travel! Go with the flow. You just have to be open, have a good heart, and trust in the Universe. You will be supported with whatever you desire. So what do you have to offer the world? XoXo.

5 p.m. – I just finished reporting with the monk. He's half Thai, half German. His energy is so calming, and you can just tell how wise he is when he speaks. He always starts by asking, "How are you today? How was your practice?"

"I'm noticing my mind is in the future a lot. I'm thinking about what I'm going to do when I'm done with this course, or where I'm going to go. I think whether I am going to do the ten days or twenty-six. Then I tell myself I am only staying for today. I am just doing one day at a time. This helps keep me in the present."

"Can you sit the whole thirty minutes, or do you move?" he asked me.

"I've sat still maybe two times during the whole thirty minutes. Other times I open my eyes, see the clock, and say, 'Seeing, seeing, seeing.' Then I close my eyes again."

"Okay, I want you to notice that you want to open your eyes before you open them and say, 'Intending to open my eyes, intending to open my eyes.' Catch yourself before you do it."

Then I said, "I find myself still attached to someone in my past. They keep coming in my thoughts, and I don't want them to." He basically told me to notice when it happens. Ugh! Thinking constantly about someone from my past who I've chosen not to be a part of my future for a reason. But he comes up in my mind during meditation, in the shower, anywhere doing anything. Thinking of different scenarios, if I do see him again, I wouldn't want to get taken advantage of or feel disrespected by him. This would cause weakness in me, and I don't want to let him affect me after I've worked so hard to repair myself and get him out of my mind!!

I want to learn more about the Buddha. It's amazing how one person can create a religion—Buddha, Jesus… I am thinking, what if our generation became a part of a new religion? One that everyone can be part of and not be "separated." "Love" of people together. But I don't even want it to be a "religion." People can just be it.

I'm sweating, it's so hot. If I could eat anything right now it would be a Dairy Queen ice cream cake! Maybe I'll spend my birthday this year in Canada so I can have one. LOL. The year both my parents bought me a large size Dairy Queen cake was the best. It was the one time where I was actually happy that they didn't talk. LOL. :p Gotta love life! Kisses. Almost done Day 4! Whoopee!!

9:15 p.m. – Came in early. It has been a long day, and I really wanted to write. First off, my lower back is aching, has been on and off for about two days, mostly when I bend over.

Yesterday morning I felt nauseous and thought it may be from the coconut oil I drank before breakfast. I'm still bloated. Two days ago when my stomach was really big, I put my hands on it and it was like as if I had a baby! I am hoping it will go down soon. I haven't been eating much —bananas for breakfast, then lunch. That's it.

I went to the outdoor "wishing Buddha" as I do almost every day so far. I put an incense between my praying hands and prayed to God, Jesus, and Buddha. I ask that my life be healed from when I was four years old and that all my sins be forgiven. I ask for God's forgiveness of all my wrongdoing and to help me forgive others who have hurt me and caused me pain. I also ask for forgiveness of those I may have hurt as well. Then I say thank you and light the incense and put it in the bowl with the rest of them. As I watch the flame on the incense, I imagine my life being purified. ♥

Then, during sitting meditation tonight, I was brought down a dark tunnel, and when I hit the bottom, I was in a dark hole. "This is what the Universe is, a dark hole." These words came to me as a knowingness. "The Universe is a dark hole, and it is in your eyes." As I got an image of eyes and the black pupils inside them. "Your eyes are a reflection of the Universe." I then thought of every animal, bug, human, et cetera, has black specs in their eyes, black circles, just like black holes. Interesting.

Right after that, I got an image of chicken fingers. Then chicken fingers with plum sauce to go with it. Why am I thinking of chicken fingers? I don't even eat meat anymore. I then thought of cooking them in my oven at home; I used to love them. I thought of where they came from, M&M's Meat Shop in my small hometown, and I was in the store remembering the times my mom would bring us there. I'd drink the peach juice or raspberry juice in the back corner, and my mom would order boxes of food. M&M's pizzas were the best; we lived off of them! All of a sudden a trail of memories came in of everything my mom's done for me.

- Packing the van, so on the last day of school we'd be ready to head to camp for the summer.
- Bringing us to church in the mornings before school.
- Taking us to countless dentist appointments on River Street. She was there for my wisdom teeth getting taken out.
- Buying me eggnog at Christmas time because she knew I loved it and it made me happy.

- Bringing us to dance classes at Miss Anna's and spending hours getting our dresses and uniforms fitted by the complex.
- The Canada Games Complex. Babysitting, swimming lessons, diving.
- Driving us to soccer. Driving, driving, driving.
- Getting family photos done across the street from Shear Heaven, our family-run hair salon.
- Doing our hair. Cutting it, styling it, dealing with us in her chair. All she wanted was to make us happy.
- Playing fetch with Belle, our little Yorkshire terrier. Walking to Tim Hortons. Hiding Belle in my winter coat in Tim Hortons as we sipped on hot chocolate.
- Being there when I had a seizure; coming to the hospital with me.
- Rubbing my back when I'd cough in the kitchen sink. She took care of me when I had pneumonia for months and was hospitalized.
- Making homemade delicious potato and lentil soup.
- Writing us birthday cards, no matter where we were in the world.
- Teaching me how to ride a two-wheel bike. I remember waving to her to come out and help me as she was doing the dishes near the window.
- Planting flowers and going flower shopping with her, buying hanging flower pots.
- Visiting me in Vancouver, walking to Kits Beach.
- Buying me my colorful bedspread when I first moved to London for college. She got me settled in residence.
- Letting me use her credit card to buy Skype minutes so I could call her.
- Teaching me how to do Highlights for Hope on mannequins in the upstairs washroom of our home so I could help her raise money for cancer.
- Getting me ready for my graduations and taking pictures of me.
- Going on road trips across the USA and driving home from college.

- Sponsoring my massage school when I really wanted to sign up, and for buying me my first massage table that we drove to the US border to pick up. I still use it ten years later.

As these memories flooded in (some came as I was writing now), I began to cry. I was so overwhelmed with the amount of love and care my mother has given me. She loves me so much. I am so grateful to have her as a mother. Mom, if you ever read this, I want you to know I love you so much. Your life as a mother has really shown me what it truly means to love. You have gone above and beyond. My life I live now is yet a reflection of the love you have given me. You have taught me everything I know. Please don't ever doubt yourself for a moment. I know that God is just as proud of you as I am. And I hope one day, when I have a little girl, that I will pass on what you have given me. I want to make you happy, I want to make you proud, and I want to take care of you for the rest of your life.

I love you, Mama. You will always be in my heart forever and always, XoXo

Be Good!

Love, your Baba Girl, your Angel, and your chi chi.

Amanda ♥♥♥

Sunday, June 7, 2015

Vipassana Day 5

5:20 p.m. - I just gave myself a haircut. I put my hair in a braid right before I had to report with the teacher, and when I came out I looked at the end of my braid and it was scraggly and thin, only a few hairs were longer than the rest. This has got to go, I said to myself. So I went to my room, took out the scissors, cut the scraggly ends off, then flipped my hair over, grabbed the ends in my left hand then cut with my right. Took about an inch off. I haven't cut my hair since beginning of November 2013. I got it cut right before I went to Thailand the first time; I think when I get out of here I will treat myself to a professional haircut. Too bad Mama's not around! I guess I could wait till October or November when she comes to Asia.

I've lost 1.4 kilograms since I got here, I have no idea how much that is in pounds, but at least it's something! I want to get back to my normal weight, 123 to 125 pounds. Right now I am focusing on my mind, tuning it up. Then I can focus on my body.

This morning I got up at 4 a.m., did some yoga in my room, then went to the meditation hall at 4:45 a.m. The hall literally is a kingdom. It's a gorgeous white temple with two floors and a wraparound porch. It is where I learn, every day, studying my mind. Meditating, thinking, bowing to Buddha, walking, thinking, meditating, sitting, looking, seeing, hearing, noticing. This morning after walking meditation, I sat down but was exhausted. I went into child's pose and slept for a half an hour. When I woke up it was almost time for breakfast. I ate corn, lettuce, and bean sprouts. Noodle soup was the main dish, but I just don't like eating spicy noodles for breakfast. I'm thinking of asking if I can just have a plate of fruit.

After lunch, I lay down, drank hot water with honey, then meditated beside the big golden stupa. I was able to sit for thirty-five minutes without moving. My mind still wanders a lot, thinking of the past and future. Most men I've been intimate with came up as well. Some good thoughts that I indulge in; others, not so much. Thought about the players and the experiences I went through with them while getting caught being untruthful. I try to have compassion for them and don't hold anger. I just wouldn't go back to them. My standards are rising; no more players! No more being disrespected and lied to. :)

Well, my time's up to forty minutes now, so I better get with it. I want to meditate in my room. There are no distractions. Going to get more tea, then I will practice. I am here to practice so I can teach others. What I am learning is very valuable. I must take full advantage of my time here and dedicate myself with a lot of discipline. I am ready to transform my life. Let's do this, girl! XoXo. Time for bed.

If I write a book about this twenty-six-day meditation experience, I want it to be called *Falling Mangoes*. Being aware of every moment. Yesterday when I was washing my hands outside, a mango fell from a huge tree just a few feet away from me. I looked up to see a squirrel running through the tree. Tonight when I started my walking meditation beside the outdoor stupa, I put my hand on top of my head when I saw two squirrels chasing each other through the gigantic mango tree. As soon as I passed it, a loud smash came from right behind me. Yep, a falling mango! If anyone ever got hit or gets hit (let's hope not), it would really hurt!! You must be aware of every moment when you are meditating. Not thinking about the past or the future. Even though it's inevitable, you can train your mind to come back to the present. It just takes a lot of work. The falling mangoes are a good representation of life; sometimes it seems like things are smashing down around us, and chaos erupts. But it's during these moments in time, when chaos strikes, that we are tested on how great our ability to keep our inner peace is. This is why we call meditation a practice. It's a gateway to help us in our everyday life to deal with the outer circumstances that we may have no control over in a way that doesn't disturb our inner peace. To be aware, acknowledge, and to breathe through it, knowing "this too shall pass." Living in the present moment is everything; it's the only thing that exists. Right here, right now. I just did forty minutes sitting and walking. I'm very proud of myself. ♥

Monday, June 8, 2015

Vipassana Day 6

I just finished meditation in my room. The bell rang for lunch two minutes ago. I meditated four and a half hours this morning, and it's only 10:30 a.m. I went to the hall at 4:10 a.m., then had three little bananas for breakfast, and again, they had noodles. I started meditating in my room at 7:30 a.m., starting with sitting. I found being in my room is less distracting, having no people around, but my thoughts are getting louder. It was definitely harder to concentrate. When I sat on my bed, I ended up looking at the time and just wanted to sleep. I lay down halfway through my meditation. Then two minutes later, a black cat came from under my bed, jumped up, then started walking against my body. I guess he is a sign I need to sit back up. So I did, and I finished my meditation. Discipline is key! Between sittings, I washed my white clothes in a bucket in the bathroom. I do all my laundry by hand. My room is very simple—a bed, a side table, and a fan on the wall. I only have my main necessities out, and I just have very minimal white clothes.

Being simple is easy. I like it. Time for lunch, then have to finish my eleven hours before reporting with the teacher monk. I've done six hours and forty minutes of mediating already this morning. Xo.

3:30 p.m. – I just went to town on cleaning my washroom. After having a shower and washing more clothes in the bucket, I got on my hands and knees and started scrubbing the floor. I poured bathroom cleaner product on the floor, walls, toilet, and sink. I swear I scrubbed out years' worth of dirt from between the tiles. I was thinking of nothing else but scrubbing and washing away the dirt, watching it go down the drain. They say the outer world is a reflection of your inner world. It's as if I was cleaning my mind and polishing my thoughts as I cleared away the old dirt.

Totally in the zone. I had just finished forty minutes of sitting meditation. I am already feeling more productive and focused. My heart and soul are present, working together; I can just feel it. I'm going to go to my meeting soon. I will do a walking meditation first by the stupa. :) After I drink another milk. :) I am feeling very calm. I feel like I'm meditating as I write; it's so peaceful. The fan feels so good on my skin, and I feel so good after having a shower. I believe meditation is the key to success. I want to teach it around the world.

I keep thinking how Grandad said that I need to write a book about my experiences and that Oprah will interview me. I seriously think he has natural abilities as well. By far the smartest guy I know. Why? Because he's traveled the world! He has been my inspiration since I was a little girl, and it makes me so happy that he supports and believes in me. ♥

5:50 p.m. – Just got back to my room. I went to my meeting and was given a profound teaching. I bowed three times to Buddha, then the monk.

> **Monk:** Amanda, how was your day?
>
> **Me:** My morning meditation was difficult. I had many negative thoughts that just trailed on. After a few minutes I would notice them and then focus on breathing or on my feet.
>
> **Monk:** Did you use kindness, love, and compassion?
>
> **Me:** No, I didn't think of that. I just was aware of them.
>
> **Monk:** Use what the Buddha taught. Send kindness, love, and compassion. You need to forgive. Forgive those who have hurt you. You need to let go of the attachment of the emotion of the memory. The memory will always be there. It is the action you take when the memory comes that matters. You can't control the memory, but you can control your action. If you forgive, you will no longer suffer when thoughts arise. *Forgiveness is key to end suffering.*
>
> **Me:** Thank you. When did you start meditating?
>
> **Monk:** Since I was eleven.
>
> **Me:** Who taught you?
>
> **Monk:** A monk in Bangkok. Now practice for forty-five minutes, focus on rising, falling, meditating, touching (right lower back body, then left lower back body).

His answer was so bang-on. How did I not realize I needed to forgive the people who have kept coming in my thoughts for months and years! I am the one who has been suffering, not them, because I have not let go, I have not forgiven. The pain is still in me, so whenever memories or thoughts arise, it is I who suffers.

I saw a sparkle at the bottom of my thumb. Guess I'm on the right track. Thank you, angels, for showing your presence. After I left the meeting, I went to the wishing Buddha to pray. I grabbed an incense and placed it between my praying hands.

"In the name of the Father, the Son, and the Holy Spirit, Amen. Thank you, God, Jesus, and Buddha for this day. I am so grateful. Please help me forgive those who have hurt me. I want to be free from suffering and pain. I am ready to forgive; please help me. Also please purify my life of when I was six years old. I ask for your forgiveness to everyone I may have hurt and for me to forgive everyone who hurt or were mean to me. Please forgive me if I have sinned. I ask to be cleansed, healed, and forgiven for everything from when I was six years old. Thank you, thank you, God. May I forgive and be forgiven. May the angels dance around me and may the heavens watch over me as I make everyone up there proud. XoXo Amanda

11 p.m. – After witnessing the falling mangoes, I wondered how they get them down. The mango trees are enormous! After praying at the wishing Buddha earlier, I was sitting just watching everything around me. A dog was rolling in the sand beside the stupa. Butterflies were fluttering by, there was a big, bright white cloud surrounded by gray ones. A man walked by with a long stick with a wooden, wrapped handle on its end and he had a green basket in the other hand. He then walked to where the cars were parked, lifted the long stick in the air, and low and behold, he got a mango in the basket! Aha! Now I know how they pick the mangoes. Then he climbed the tree, so high I couldn't even see him. He brought the green basket with him too. What a trouper. A true barefooted Thai mango picker! I thought about what if the tree branch snapped but was assured he's been up this certain tree many times. If I wasn't in my practice, I would have asked if I could join him. Thai mangoes are delicious—*aroy* means tasty in Thai.

A guy from Russia started speaking to me beside the outdoor stupa where I had been taking a break between walking and sitting meditation. It was very interesting conversation, I don't regret it. I learned he was living in Phuket, Thailand, for four years. We talked all night; it was his third ten-day sitting here. He taught me a ritual his friend learned in Nepal. "Walk around the stupa, lighting a candle on all four sides, then walk around three times. Pray to light the path to enlightenment for yourself and everyone in the world." He also gave me some tea from India. We talked about past lives, spirit, yoga, meditation, among other spiritual things. I'm happy we talked, even though we broke the rules. *Yolo.*

Tuesday, June 9, 2015

Vipassana Day 7

My vision is foggy, and my head is throbbing. I am aware, but my state is extremely altered. My right eye is cloudy. I feel light, peaceful, and am telling myself not to worry. I just had the deepest state of meditation since I've been here. I sat for forty-five minutes without opening my eyes. I focused on my belly rising and falling with my breath three times, then I noticed I was sitting, saying it three times. Then I said *knowing* on each inhale three times, then focused on touching my lower right back, then the left side. Pain in my back started coming, and I just said *acknowledging*, then continued on my point of focus. I learned to do this during Goenka's meditation. Goenka is a man who spread another type of Vipassana Meditation around the world. I highly recommend in doing his ten-day silent meditation course as there are centers all around the world. It is very popular and a great investment in yourself to do. So during my time when the pain came up in my body, I didn't move, I just was aware of the pain, then it faded away.

When my alarm went off, I put my hands in prayer and said, "Thank you, God, for this practice, and thank you, Amanda, for this practice." I bowed three times mindfully to Buddha, then went outside. After one of today's meditation, I saw a double rainbow! I knew it was a gift from God. I love rainbows, and I know God gave me one to show his presence and that he is proud of me. I am proud of me too. In that moment, I knew I was on the right path. My heart was happy. Then I went to drink two glasses of water. Feeling very relaxed and in an altered state, as I had said.

Then I got a cup of hot water to mix with honey. My vision began to blur while walking to my room. I'm still very light-headed. Continued headache and feeling cloudy. I am going to ask the teacher why this happens when I get a chance.

Last night and today, I was slacking on meditation. I felt so peaceful, I just wanted to sit around. When I tried sitting after lunch, I opened my eyes after twenty minutes. I was restless and felt down on myself that I couldn't do it. Time was going by slowly. I had compassion for myself as I was thinking whether I'd be able to complete twenty-six days. I told myself only today, stay one day. ♥ Resting now.

11 p.m. – I still have a bad headache. This isn't normal for me. I never get headaches. My writing isn't even clean like it usually is. I'm so tired. I'm always tired after breakfast and lunch. I hope my headache goes away. I need to sleep. Maybe my body's not used to not eating in the afternoon. I'm hungry. When I got back to my room, my lock wasn't even on properly. It was on the door handle.

Tonight was a ceremony for Buddha. We did chanting, then a few hundred people walked around the stupa and temple three times with one lit candle, three lit incense, and one rose. It was cool to be a part of it. Just my headache wasn't fun. I don't know why it still hurts. I miss my mama. I hope she has a good time at the Highlights for Hope ten-year anniversary. It will be ten years tomorrow, June 10. Wow. That's a decade. Such a special day tomorrow. HFH has been a part of our life in a major way, I ♥ my MOM!!! HFH 4ever!

11:45 p.m. – I just jumped out of bed and went outside my door and sat on the floor. My left arm was tingling, maybe because I was sleeping on it. The sensation made me anxious, and I wanted to be outside my room in case I needed help. Scary. I ate two bananas. I'm going to go back to sleep, so tired. Don't have a headache anymore, just slight worry. I sometimes get paranoid about having another seizure because I remember the two that I had so clearly. That's why any body tingles make me anxious, but I'm sure I was just sleeping on my arm in a different position. I'm grateful I've never experienced a seizure since I was around twelve years old. Time to fall back asleep, I'm okay. Good night.

Wednesday, June 10, 2015

Vipassana Day 8

10 p.m. – Today is a very special day! Tenth anniversary for Highlights for Hope!!!

I am so proud of my mom for all of her hard work, dedication, and passion for helping others. We have helped raised a lot of money for cancer and have brought hope and happiness to many lives by weaving pink highlight extensions into supporters' hair. Today I wear my Highlights for Hope for my auntie Carolyn. She is the reason Highlights for Hope exists. I love and miss her so much. The pink highlights have brought light during dark times. I am so grateful to be a part of something so beautiful. Highlights for Hope will always be in my heart. We have raised over $100,000 by putting in the pink highlights and it's been an incredible journey! I am blessed to have my mom and am grateful for everything she has done in my life. I prayed at the Buddha shrine tonight to celebrate Highlights for Hope's ten-year anniversary and lit an incense in honor of everyone who has been touched by cancer. I love you, Mom. XoXo.

Today was, well, terrific!! Kind of. I slept in because I still had a headache when I woke up. I skipped breakfast then meditated at 8 a.m. I found it difficult to concentrate, as my mind was running on wheels. Lunch was yummy: watermelon, lychees, spicy peas and tofu, potatoes, and rice, with popcorn for dessert! I had my report and told the monk about my cloudy vision from last night. He said to not get attached to what I see, and I can look up what it represents by searching Vipassana side effects. I walked around the stupa for fifty minutes at night, then sat for fifty minutes, but my mind was in the future the whole time, thinking about my visa run and what I'm going to do this summer. Bedtime, Mandy's sleepy.

XoXo

Tuesday, June 11, 2015

Vipassana Day 9

9:50 p.m. – After just finishing my last walking meditation for the night, I went to the washroom and saw a new spider on the wall. I said to myself, "You're replacing the cockroach." I hadn't seen the cockroach since my first night. Looking around the sink, with a thought maybe he was in the sink, I said in my head: "Well, I guess he's gone!" As soon as I said that I looked down at my feet to see two long antennae. "Oh, my god! I thought you were gone!!" I said. As I jumped off the toilet, he ran behind it. I looked to make sure I wasn't seeing things. Yup, it was him. I got out of the bathroom, shut the door, and started writing on my bed, with that black cat that always sneaks in my room. He's licking his body and just laying on my bed. I don't really want the cockroach in my bathroom. I'm not in the mood to try to catch it though. Zenned out and tired.

So during my last walking meditation, about ten minutes in, I thought of Jim Carrey on *Oprah*. How he went to the top of a mountain overlooking the Hollywood sign, seeing himself as a movie star. He wrote a check for himself worth ten million dollars and ended up getting that amount for *Dumb and Dumber*. I then said, "Thinking, thinking, thinking." We are supposed to say that three times when we catch ourselves thinking. Then I said, "Focus, focus, focus." I felt like my situation would be the same as Jim Carrey's. I continued walking, and when I brought my right heel up, I said "love" in my head. My words did not want to say "toes, lifting, moving, stepping" like I had been. Then I thought of five million, then all of a sudden, a new mantra for my walking began. "Fifty (toes) million (lifting) of my books are (moving) selling (stepping)."

I repeated this over and over, focusing on each step. Then I realized I was walking for a total of fifty minutes. There's a reason for everything! I started seeing "Fifty million copies sold, by: Amanda Ruberto" at the bottom of a book. Dreams come true when you really want them to. Then I was imagining Oprah interviewing me, and I thought how she was the first thing I crossed off on my dream board. And in high school and college, I would always look forward to watching her show at 4 p.m. She was and still is one of my idols. :)

I had to ask the head monk who organizes the international students if I could use my phone to call my mom to send me money so I could extend my visa. I hadn't saved money for my travels, as I flew to Japan on complete faith and intuition and then ended up in Thailand doing exactly what I intended to do. To help teach yoga and meditation! So I called my mom and asked if she could help me a bit so I could extend my visa to stay in the country so I could complete my course. I told her about how my experience is going and what it's like in the temple. She is going to send me $200 tomorrow for my visa, thank God!! I am going to complete the twenty-six days for sure now! I felt like I was slacking a bit the last three days, but now I'm back on track. I was even offered a ride back to Bangkok today by the monk's dad who I was originally supposed to catch the bus with from Chiang Rai to Chiang Mai, and then luckily saw him at the bus station. He was inspired that I was doing the course and ended up signing up for the twenty-six-day course too, but as a monk. It was nice to have someone there that I knew a little bit. We'd only really see each other in the dining hall, though, as the monks meditated in different temples than the international students. So when his dad came to pick him up, thinking the course was done after ten days, he told his father he was staying longer to complete the twenty-six-days. But when his father found me and asked if I wanted a ride to Bangkok that day, I thought what an escape to freedom that would be. My intention before arriving was only to do the ten days. I actually felt ready to go. Then the son said to me that we can't give up. He was right. Freedom is here and now. This place frees us from the real prison—our minds. His father left and I went back into my practice to dive deeper into my meditation and I'm so glad I did.

XoXo

Friday, June 12, 2015

Vipassana Day 10

7:40 a.m. – I just finished eating corn and drinking Sissy Delight tea for breakfast. I came on my computer to see if my mom's transaction came through. I noticed there are no credit cards linking to my profile. Where did it go? Did my papa (dad) pay it off? Feeling shocked and relieved, I feel an immense emotion of gratitude. The power of forgiveness. When finances come up in meditation, I forgive myself and my papa. I sent love and compassion. Still trying to figure out what really happened, wondering if he'd have the authority to cancel my credit card. It crossed my mind maybe the bank sent it to collections. Then I opened my checking account to see the account balance: $-16.78 and funds on hold: $7,188.71. Aha, that's where it is. What's *funds on hold*? I clicked on the information button… Funds on hold are deposits you have made to your account that have not yet been cleared by the bank.

View Account Holds – Checking
Hold Type: Branch Hold
Start Date: Mar 18, 2015
Available Date: Jun 13, 2015
Amount: $7,188.71 CAD

Total Amounts of Holds: $7,188.71 CAD

Holds will be removed from your account by approximately 6 a.m. on the Available Date.

Wow. He actually did. I am so happy. Words cannot express how much this means to me. March 18th, I was still in Toronto. I did talk to him on the phone about it then. He said he would help me, but he didn't tell me he'd made any action. It's funny how I see this the day before the transaction is about to go through. I'm crying with an overwhelming sense of gratefulness, from the bottom of my heart. I feel a huge block has been removed from my life and believe this has created a gateway of abundance to flow in.

Beautiful music is playing outside. I feel so good. I am going to sweep my room and the outside balcony, then I will meditate, all day. Always do your best. Practice, practice, practice. Never give up. Love you, Papa.

XoXo Amanda

Saturday, June 13, 2015

Vipassana Day 11

6 p.m. – I got permission to go get my visa extended at a local visa office. First thing I had to do was take some money out, and after trying a third ATM at a convenience store nearby, I thanked the Lord the machine worked and money came out. I took out 4,000 baht, which is $146; 1,900 baht will go to extending my visa for a month. The other half of the money will have to cover me for Bangkok. It's not much, but I'm not worried. I'm happy to have money for the bus. Thank you, Mommy, for supporting me. This Vipassana course isn't easy. After talking to two meditators about four or five nights ago while having a tea break, it kinda made me not care as much. I began taking breaks often and haven't been meditating back-to-back. I still wasn't 100 percent sure if I was going to stay ten or twenty-six days. I wanted to do twenty-six, but my focus just vanished. I had to use my phone to call my mom, and then they gave me my computer as well.

When I drove to the convenience store with a guy from the temple, I was thinking how my mind is weak because I haven't been disciplined to meditate. I then saw a big poster of Master in someone's garage as we drove by. I took this as a reminder of why I am doing this course and it reminded me that Master told my monk friend's dad that I have a strong mind three days prior.

He is right. I do have a really strong mind, and I am so happy that Master believes in me! ♥

Not going to lie, I've been on my computer a lot. I needed it to do my online banking and call my mom with skype. However I just haven't given it back yet and I've been reading the news, researching about foods I'm eating, reading about successful authors like Paulo Coelho and Elizabeth Gilbert. They are both role models to me. I was also on Oprah's network, and I read an article a friend sent to me about meditation. I am truly not into it anymore. I was doing great, ten hours a day. Now it's less than five. :s But!!! There is still hope.

There are still seventeen days left, which is more than enough time to get back on track and focused. I have all my visa forms filled out, a passport photo, my passport, and the money needed to apply for a month's extension. I had been focusing on getting it all sorted the last three days, so now it's done. I just have to go to the immigration office Monday or Tuesday. I will give back my phone and computer too, since it's distracting me and I don't need them anymore. I am expected to meditate eleven to twelve hours a day now. How hardcore is that! Seriously!! I can do it, though. My mind may have gotten off track, and I wondered if I should just go, but I'm not going to give up. I can get back into this. My transformation isn't over.

I was feeling earlier like I was in a jail. The food was just not up to means. In other words, I didn't like it, even today's breakfast and lunch. Breakfast was a bowl of noodles, like Mr. Noodles, with a side of cracker sticks. At lunch when I saw a bowl of lettuce, my heart was jumping up and down. I was sooo happy! First time having salad in so long. When I got to the bowl to serve myself, I realized there was no dressing, just lettuce with cucumbers. Wishing there was olive oil and vinegar; there wasn't. Even though it was plain, I remained humble for the food I was given. Having lettuce and cucumber was enough for me. I didn't eat the other dishes with tofu and spiced eggs mixed with who knows what. I was definitely missing the food at Rai Cherntawan—unlimited amount of fruit, veggies, and I could make my own salad.

This place also sometimes feels like a mental institution. Then I tell myself it is. We are all here to work on our minds. Once you check in, you can't go out. White clothes at all times, "no eye contact, no talking" is what the head monk for the international students repeats to us daily. I can do this, though. My mind will get stronger. I will succeed. Come on, Amanda, get back in the game! You're a trouper. Twelve hours a day isn't bad! Ha! Ya, right! LOL. Okay, it's a little extreme, but it's possible. Just do it. When you finish walking, sit right away. When you finish sitting, walk right away. Phra Ajarn Nawi, the head monk of the Wat Ram Poeng, said the more I meditate, the less sleep I'll need—four to six hours. He said he sleeps two to four hours. I asked if when he sleeps two hours if he's tired the next day, and he said, "Yes, and I get tired from six hours too." Guess it doesn't really make a difference.

I saw a guy's sheet today and saw he meditated for fourteen hours yesterday. He's done the twenty-six-day course before. This guy's full on. He's always sitting in the left corner, facing the Buddha. My friend who I met while I was registering for the course and encouraged me to do the twenty-six-days hasn't been in the temple library the past two days. I'm sure he's doing well. And the other European girl is always in the temple. I wonder how she stays so with it! I need to get with the program. Sixteen days will fly by, so give it what you got, girl! XoX Mandy

9:30 p.m. – I just had two amazing meditations. I walked for one hour on my gorgeous porch, then sat for one hour, until 9 p.m. I didn't even open my eyes. I was focused the whole time. A few thoughts came up here and there, but for the most part I rocked it :) I'm feeling calm and relaxed. Then I made some tea with hot water and went to the outdoor wishing Buddha. I prayed, "Dear Jesus, thank you for taking care of my family for another day. Thank you for taking care of Samantha, Amanda, Rudy, Cody, Mommy, Papa, Belle, and Bailey. A special thank-you for today.

Thank you for the food I ate, the tea I am drinking, the money that will help extend my visa, for my mom for supporting me, for not giving up, for you giving me the strength to keep going, and for my wonderful practice tonight. Please forgive me of my sins when I was eleven. Please purify my life and heal me where there is hurt. I ask for forgiveness of others who I may have hurt as well. Thank you, God, for purifying my life."

I lit an incense and four candles, then drank my tea. I am also grateful to whoever paid off my credit card. The funds on hold went through today. I am officially free from my credit card debt. Thank you, God. I am ready for abundance. ♥ The cat is sleeping in my room again tonight, I named him Shadow because when he walked beside me during meditation, that's all I saw, his shadow. ♥

Sunday, June 14, 2015

Vipassana Day 12

I did not write in my journal on this day.

Monday, June 15, 2015

Vipassana Day 13

What a day...halfway through the course. I am happy I'm still here. This morning I got a ride to the immigration office in Chiang Mai. Right before, I asked a kitchen staff member if I could have fruit for breakfast, and veggies and salad for lunch. I was really not feeling the noodles for breakfast, and vegetarian bacon strips and tofu at lunch. Doesn't work well for me and my stomach.

When I got to the office I noticed a babe. I ended up sitting beside him and was there for five hours. He is from San Francisco and played rugby for Berkley while studying business. Turned out he's going to Burning Man this year. Burning Man is a weeklong art festival in the Black Rock Desert in Nevada, US, where a large community creates a temporary city involving selfless giving of one's unique talents for the enjoyment of all. He showed me a picture of him and his roommates who just got their Burning Man outfits at last night's Sunday Night Market. I told him about my meditation course, and he said he's wanted to do a Vipassana. He's actually going to Bangkok tomorrow for a five-day acro yoga course! How sweet is that?! If I wasn't meditating, I for sure would have gone.

I got my thirty-day visa extension after a long wait. Didn't feel long, though, I meditated for parts of it, as my new friend read *Shantaram* on his Kindle. "Amanda Ruberto from Wat Rampoeng" announced on the intercom. When I got to the counter, one of the immigration officials had his palms in his lap and eyes closed. He was meditating!! LOL. He looked up at me and smiled, and I used my hand to zip my mouth closed, showing I couldn't talk either. Silence. Ha ha. I then full-on taught him how to meditate. I said, "Hands on your lap. Raise your left hand, rising, rising, rising, moving, moving, moving, turning, turning, turning, lowering, lowering, lowering, touching, touching, touching. Now the right hand, rising, rising, rising..."

He copied everything I did. "Now breathing into your stomach...rising, falling, rising, falling..." I taught him the technique I had been learning.

"Thank you so much!" he said. "I will teach the other staff." Then I showed him a picture of V. Vajiramehdi and I. I invited him to Rai Cherntawan to come learn more. He loved it! As I was walking out, Maria, the woman who was doing the same course walked in! She just finished her ten-day retreat yesterday, and I never got a chance to say good-bye. She and her husband were getting re-entry visas because they are going back to India June 29, then back to Chiang Mai to live. I was happy I got to see her again and am definitely going to keep in touch.

Tonight I went to the wishing Buddha and said my prayers. I asked for forgiveness of my sins from when I was thirteen years old. I then purified myself with a lit incense and put it in the pot with the others. Then I attended the ceremony for Lord Buddha Day. Did some chanting in the beautiful temple, then walked around the outdoor pagoda three times. I lit my candle for Nepal. I prayed dearly for them. I asked the heavens to open the sky and shine light and love down on everyone who has been affected by the earthquakes.

When I got back to my room, I checked my Facebook. Today was my first day on it, and the first thing I saw on my news feed was my friend Angie's engagement! I cried, I was so happy. Then I saw pictures of Highlights for Hope tenth-anniversary party, cried again, and checked all my family members' pages. Checking Facebook today and seeing what my loving family and friends have been up to made me so emotional. Full of happiness, love, and gratitude. I bawled.

That was this afternoon, but this evening I got a Facebook message from a hair school for beauty professionals that I had signed up for and had decided to drop out to travel the world to learn more about meditation, yoga, and helping people in need as I went along. She said if I don't respond by June 20, they would send my file to collections. I called my friend Joe right away, and we talked for an hour. I sent a message back to the woman from the school, basically asking if there is any money left over that they can give me from the $250 deposit. I only attended a week of school, so doesn't make sense I have to pay $6,000. Pretty ridiculous. *Shanti, shanti.* It will sort out, no need to stress. I am a divine human being who has come to serve the world. Do not forget who you are. You are doing amazing things, Amanda. Just keep following your heart and the Universe will support you. You will save many lives. Focus on yourself right now. This is critical. You need all of your attention on you. Mind development, it's what you came here for.

Do not get distracted by outdoor actions. Just listen within and the answers will come. You will know what to do. No need to worry. Just be happy and live free.

XoXo Amanda ♥

Tuesday, June 16, 2015

Vipassana Day 14

10 p.m. – It's *official*! I'm going to the Dalai Lama's eightieth birthday!!! *Yahoooo*! I am so so so soooooooooo *excited*! ☺ I just booked my flight from Bangkok to LA, arriving on the Fourth of July. My friend Emma bought my plane ticket *and* a ticket to his birthday event as a gift. Wow.

Honestly, a dream come true. I have been sleeping with my "List of Dreams" for the year, under my pillow the last few nights. I would read it over and over. I even placed the paper on my heart and focused on "breathing" it into my body, making it a part of me. My heart is beyond grateful. This is truly something very special to me. To be with Dalai Lama on his eightieth birthday is truly an honor and a blessing. Thank you to my angels and the heavens for aligning the stars. Making magic happen, every day. Sugar, sugar. ♥

Wednesday, June 17, 2015

Vipassana Day 15

I think this is the nicest writing I've ever done. I feel very calm and relaxed; I am writing very slowly. I never take my time when I write; I am actually focused on only writing and putting effort and care into it. I just saw sparkles on my page. Writing with love. I feel like I could just stop now and everything will be okay.

Thursday, June 18, 2015

Vipassana Day 16

Ten days left! Ahhh. Not going to lie, I only did two hours of walking meditation and thirty minutes of sitting. I did my laundry, cleaned my room, and wrote out things I want to do and made a loose four-year travel plan. I am very excited for this summer! Going to Dalai Lama's birthday celebration and spending the summer in LA! Then, Burning Man! There's something about LA that just makes me feel alive. So much to do, so much to see, so many beautiful and cool people to meet. I just love the lifestyle. Laid back, surfers, beaches, vegetarian and vegan restaurants. This summer's about networking but most of all, having fun! I want to get into really good shape too. Runs down Venice Beach and up Runyon Canyon. I can do yoga at the top ☺ I also want to focus on getting my websites ready for when I head out again.

4:30 p.m. – I just had my meeting with Phra Ajarn Navi. I told him I was still thinking about the future a lot. He said, "Where is your body now? Here. The present moment is what makes your future and shapes your past. Everything you do will be stored in your memory. You can change your mind over and over about what you want to do in the future. But just be here now, focus on your body. Try to only sleep four hours in the next few days. You need to get ready for your determination."

"I'll try," I said.

"You're only here for a few more days, just do it," he responded.

Not sure if it's going to happen. Ya, it'd be cool/great to not sleep for three days. Umm, okay, I'll give it a shot. I will try my best ☺ Almost liquid snack time. I'm feeling hungry! And tired... D (half moon tonight).

XoXo Amanda ♥

Friday, June 19th, 2015

Vipassana Day 17

I did not write in my journal on this day.

Saturday, June 20, 2015

Vipassana Day 18

8 a.m. – I just finished eating breakfast. I had a mango, an apple, and a banana. Prior to eating, I woke up at 6 a.m., did five sun salutations, took a big sip out of my coconut oil bottle, then drank four cups of water. I have gotten into a little routine. I am glad I'm not having noodles for breakfast anymore. I'm happy I spoke up and asked for fruit instead. One of the *meshis* (nuns) got me a big bag of apples yesterday.

I just saw angel dust to the right side of my book, sparkles in the air. I feel a sense of calmness come over me. "Thank you, angels, for showing your presence," I say in my mind. It is nice to know I am being looked after. I was actually thinking about Ed, a nine-day monk-turned-meditator. About two weeks ago, on the first Buddha Day, Maria said there was a monk with a beautiful face and that he looked like Buddha. "He's the one over there, with the arm tattoo." I looked but could only see him from the back, as he was walking in the distance. I only saw him once after that, again only a side view. He walked past me as I was entering the library. Yesterday around 4 p.m., I was having water by the water taps and a guy from the kitchen sat down beside me and said, "Hey, how are you finding it? How are you doing?" We ended up talking for about an hour.

"I was a monk here for nine days, but I left. I didn't like it too much. They chant at 4 a.m., 6:30 a.m., 1 p.m., 4 p.m., nighttime, et cetera. I left for five days, rode my bike around, did some things, then I realized I wasn't happy. I got a tarot reading, and she said the cards said I had to come back and do Determination. So I came back, but as a meditator."

Turned out, he was the monk Maria said looked like Buddha. I told him how I met Master in Japan and he invited me to Thailand. He said he had called Rai Cherntawan to see if he could ordain there, but they weren't doing it for a few weeks. I told him about Dalai Lama in the cave too, and he said "You seem to attract very high, venerable monks. Either they are attracting you, or you're attracting them." We talked about meditation, experiences, and how we feel about being here.

"The memory records everything you do, think and feel," he said. And he's right. Whatever goes on, your memory stores it. Then it re-plays random things in your life, like a TV show, and it's like you are re-experiencing it.

"What if what you think is always about when someone hurt you?" I asked.

"You say, 'I forgive you and I let go of you. Good-bye,'" he said. "Just like that." It really struck a chord. Sounded easier than I was thinking.

I believe being here has already impacted me in a positive way. I know what my triggers are. I am extra conscious of living beings, i.e., watch where I sit so I don't squish ants, sweep ants off the balcony instead of putting them in the garbage. "I'm doing this because I care about you," I said as I sweep them off the second floor. LOL.

I had a moment when after throwing my leftovers away into the black garbage bin, I almost cried. I never waste food, and here I am throwing out a tray full of it. I was thinking about Nepal that day a lot. After that, I did my own servings, switched to just eating fruits and vegetables, and haven't wasted any food since. 1) I didn't like the food. 2) The servings they gave were too much. There would be three tubs full of leftovers—just ridiculous!! I do not agree with that.

People should do their own servings or get served less. If they want more, they can go up for seconds. I am more calm and don't have energy for negativity in my life. I have lost eight pounds! After almost two years of being about ten pounds above my average, I am finally getting back to my normal self. I am feeling very good about this. I want to weigh between 120 to 123 pounds. It is really important for me to have a healthy body, and it all comes from having a healthy mind. I am looking forward to many beach days this summer at Venice Beach and California pool parties! Beverly Hills, that's where I want to be! Yeah, living in Beverly Hills. :P

I want to train a lot so I can run the Great Wall of China Marathon in May, and I want to deepen my yoga practice and get more flexible so I can do the splits! It will take a lot of determination, but I believe I can do it, and I think LA is an inspiring place for me. I'm twenty-six, and that's where I really want to spend some time. Ever since right after high school, I wanted to live in Hollywood. I remember looking up "makeup for movies" school there instead of university/college. The first year of Recreation and Leisure, I applied for a soccer summer camp leader job under the Hollywood Boulevard sign while I was doing my student placement at Parkwood Hospital, seven years ago!! Now here I am in Thailand doing a twenty-six-day meditation course! Who would have thought? Pretty cool.

The cat is sleeping on my floor. Cats are so weird. I'm feeling sleepy. Oh, another quote of wrongdoing around monks. "Don't roll your pants up. It's impolite," according to the foreign monk coordinator. I had a dream a few nights ago of arriving at Pete's house. First I walked to the top of the stairs, realized other people were living there, then I went to the back to his place. I hope he's happy I'm coming to Venice! He doesn't know yet, though. He's going to get a solid five-day heads-up. I see us having a lot of fun. Juicing, yoga, surfing, exploring :) and deep chats. It's funny how I met him because of Dalai Lama, and now I'm going to see him again because of Dalai Lama. What's up with that? LOL.

I just thought, *I should teach meditation at the Tinder office.* LOL. Seriously, I think that's what I want to do. Teach meditation all summer to offices, businesspeople, retirement/nursing homes, at parks and beaches. I can teach full time by donation, and yoga too!

Like Pete said, I need to get a business website up! Ya, girl! AmandaRuberto.com. Brilliant, ha ha. Bio, credentials, massage, yoga, meditation, energy healing. Have awesome photos and make it a fun place to be, with a hint of Zen and monk action.

Tuesday, June 23, 2015

Vipassana Day 21

Two days ago I was having great meditations. I was focused, determined, relaxed, and felt peaceful. Then memories came, and it all changed. I was angry, hurt, disappointed, and resentful. My heart began to ache, and I cried and cried. I could not meditate anymore. The pain was too strong. However, just being aware of this pain kept me in the moment, and that itself is the art of meditation. I got some tea and sat by the outdoor stupa. I cried more. Heartache is one of the hardest things to go through. I went to report and told Phra Ajarn Navi my feelings and about not wanting to meditate. He said just to acknowledge the feelings when they come, but don't get lost in them. Meditation is just knowing and feeling what you are experiencing. I haven't meditated since. Now I find myself bawling my eyes out on my bed. I talked with one of my friends and she said I am experiencing this because I haven't processed what happened in my relationship.

I have my computer again because I called my papa for Father's Day. I ended up watching videos from one of my trips. I don't know if I'm in pain because I'm missing the guy I was involved with, in pain due to hurt and resentment from my expectations not being met, or just maybe not having someone I really care about around. Don't get me wrong, I love being single. Our connection was so strong since the moment we met, and I thought he'd be in my life for a long time. He's not the kind of man I want to be with, though. I need to accept and move on.

There's just so much hurt inside of me. When you miss someone so much, but at the same time you know they are not good for you. I want to heal from all of this. I need to love myself again, do what makes me happy and have the strength to be myself completely and follow my passions and dreams. I need to let go. I learned today from the Bhikkhuni, who is a fully ordained female monastic in Buddhism, during a special Dhamma Talk, which is "cosmic law and order" and is also teachings of the Buddha, that "No one can break our hearts but ourselves. We let the people into our hearts. It's a vulnerable place."

XoXo

Wednesday, June 24, 2015

Vipassana Day 22

I did not write in my journal on this day.

Thursday, June 25, 2015

Vipassana Day 23 - Determination Day 1

Ask yourself, what is more important—computers or people? Solitare or friendship? Email or family? Connecting to Wi-Fi or connecting to nature? Surfing the web or surfing the waves? Exploring your news feed or exploring the world? Looking at a screen or looking at the sunrise? We live in a day and age where people are glued to their computers and iPhones. People are not only missing the lives of those around them, but they're missing out on their own lives as well. There is a lack of connection with a thing called life when your mind is fully occupied with what's happening on the screen. You ignore your surroundings and focus on clicking buttons while editing photos for Facebook. *I'm busy. I'm working. Don't talk to me. Leave the room and shut the door.* These are all things I've heard many, many times before. "I want to share my dreams with you." Yet, I still get ignored. I read my list anyway as the eyes of the receiver are locked to the iTunes store. "Congratulations" is the remark I get to my precious life treasures. The feelings of familiarity set in place again, an aching of the heart. Why don't you just look at me and forget about what is in your cart? The moments passed, and you were gone so fast. You had only a few minutes left to truly hear me, to talk to me, to see me, but your email was more worth your time before you left the country and me behind.

#listendonttype #humanconnection #wherediditgo #closeyourcomputer #icareaboutyoumorethanyourcomputereverwill but #wealldoit #justbeconscious #thanks

Friday, June 26, 2015

Vipassana Day 24 - Determination Day 2

7 p.m. – Just waiting for this to be over. I am so ready to leave! I am looking forward to leaving Thailand and going to Dalai Lama's birthday where I'll be surrounded by highly spirited individuals, peacemakers, and healers. They are who I need the most right now.

I do not even feel like meditating. The whole morning and afternoon I was drained. Reviving my energy with a fresh salad and fruit helped. However, I probably slept about eight hours. Honestly, I am looking forward to getting out of here. It's been an interesting experience, and I learned a lot. Two more days, and I'm done. You can do it. Amanda, don't give up.

Saturday, June 27, 2015

Vipasanna Day 25 - Determination Day 3

5:30 p.m. – I am beginning to realize my true potential. Everything my past partner has done to me has been a lesson. He is truly one of my greatest teachers. He has taught me forgiveness, having compassion, to be kind and gentle with myself, to go after my dreams, and don't listen to anybody else but myself. He has taught me anything is possible and has given me fire to travel the world by myself. Truly, sometimes things that don't turn out in your favor are blessings in disguise. Things had to happen so I could be here and realize my fullest potential of the incredible human being that I am.

- A chance to go within and nurture the little girl inside of me.

- A chance to heal my wounds and treat my scars.

- A chance to discover what I truly desire in this life.

- A chance to explore the thoughts and feelings inside of me.

- A chance to fall in love with myself, my mind, body, and spirit.

XoXo
Amanda ♥

Sunday, June 28, 2015

Vipassana Day 26 - Determination continues until afternoon...

10 a.m. – Last night I had an awesome streak of meditation! Four hours straight. Walking, sitting, walking, sitting, with very little water breaks. I find that's where a good chunk of my time went, drinking water and tea, enjoying the moments as thoughts arose and passed away. My most enjoyable moments were drinking water on a wooden stool outside one of the main temples.

There were two times where I felt complete bliss. This was directly after meditating in the library. One of the cooks just delivered my lunch. He put it on a nail that's in the wall right beside my door. I smiled at him through the window. I wonder if he's the one who delivered my breakfast this morning, which consisted of pineapple, peanuts, and lychees. When I got the breakfast bag at 6:30 a.m., I saw there was a space where you could see through my window clearly in my room. The curtain shifted a bit, the light was on, and from where the bag was placed, you could clearly see inside my room. So what was I doing when they delivered the food? Sleeping on the hardwood floor with a pink towel covering me. LOL. I was fully clothed, thank God, and I used the towel as a blanket. I put my sheets and pillow under my wooden bed frame and folded the bed cushion so I wouldn't sleep there.

My meditations were so good, I guess I fell asleep. LOL. Well, I tried to stay awake, but clearly that didn't happen. I think the hardest thing about this course for me was not sleeping in the afternoons and past 4 a.m. bell, and I wasn't able to only sleep four hours and no hours during Determination. Also, just staying here for twenty-six days was hard enough; there were times I just really wanted to go. There were days I just didn't want to meditate, I'd rather have tea and water breaks and enjoy my surroundings. I found if I got upset or had heartache during a meditation, I'd sometimes just leave the building and cry somewhere, then I wouldn't meditate for the rest of the day.

I'd feel exhausted and just want to sleep. I think it was all processing and releasing. It takes a lot of energy from you. Things I enjoyed most were afternoon reporting, getting teachings from the teachers, Navi and sometimes Suphan. Some things were very valuable lessons and the advice given has really helped me with my practice and healing, i.e., compassion and kindness are keys to forgiveness.

I also liked wearing all white. It makes me feel pure. White represents a light being so it serves as a good reminder that I am "pure light." The walking and sitting meditation techniques are great. I will definitely share this way of meditating with others. Most importantly, I learned a lot about myself. I learned what my triggers are; I learned what makes me truly happy. I am more aware of my thoughts, actions, and feelings. I learned that I have so much potential and so much to offer this world.

I made a list of things that I want to do, and everything on there is really awesome. It makes me excited about life, and I know I can make anything I want happen. I can do whatever I want in this world. Go on a roller coaster with Oprah? Why not? Couch surf at the White House, why not? Teach Justin Bieber yoga and meditation, why not? Celebrate my birthday at the tallest building in the world, who said I can't? LOL. Anything is possible when you put your mind to it!

I have more discipline. I am not eating past noon, waiting for the chantings to start while having food in front of me! Making sure my room was clean at all times, I swept pretty much every day. I tried not talking as much as possible, but I wish there was a bit more supervision for that matter. Everyone was a chatterbox. There was even a "leaving party" at 5 p.m. tea break for one of the meditators, whom I hadn't even met. Everyone was gathered at the tables, talking. My friend who I registered for the course at the same time said after that he was so mad, LOL, and then he sat by himself. I happily chatted with the fellow acquaintances, as my silence had already been broken when the Russian talked to me on the seventh or eighth day. Another girl from China snuck out to KFC for chicken at night; she also killed mosquitos right in front of Suphan, one of the teachers. Her reason:

"It was going to bite me!" LOL. That's a big no-no, especially in front of the head monk at reporting.

My other friend who was a local Thai guy had a massage booked on his third day into the meditation course, LOL. He tried to go to it, but the monk in charge of the foreigners was at the main gate at the time. So he missed his massage, and he left on Day 8. A guy from Germany was supposed to do twenty-six days. He started the same day as me and left on Day 9. I could feel he was having a hard time. Then there was the hard-core meditator who was up to fifteen hours a day by the tenth day, LOL. The talkative girl from China whose room is down the hall from mine told me she went to the library at 3 a.m. and the hard-core guy was in there. One day when he came into reporting, I just started laughing (in my head), he just had hard-core written all over him. I admire his determination, focus, and hard work, but it was too much for me, LOL. Great job though, bud. He definitely succeeded his second time around…

11 a.m. – My salad has been sitting in front of me for an hour, and we just started the chantings.

11:05 a.m. – Finally, I get to eat. "Patience, patience, patience, feeling, feeling, feeling." I will definitely not miss having to wait to eat and wait for people to finish chanting before I could start.

3 p.m. – I am a powerful human being with unlimited potential. I did it! I successfully accomplished twenty-six days of Vipassana meditation. I feel purified and enlightened.

During my last sitting, for the last five minutes I was laughing hysterically. All I heard were words from Master, things he said to me before. His sense of humor has led me to reach enlightenment, I was literally rolling around on the ground, laughing my head off! Then the beeper went off. *Beep beep, beep beep, beep beep.* I couldn't have completed this course on a more magnificent note.

Thank you, Master, thank you for everything. Thank you for believing in me, supporting me, and loving me. You changed my destiny. I couldn't have done this without you. It was a miracle that we met. You were truly the answer to my prayers. I am honored and blessed to have you in my life. I look forward to see what the future has in store for us.

♥ Amanda, "Amandy," Madre.

XoXo

Monday, June 29th, 2015

Reflections

Now it's time for my Facebook update!

June 29, 2015 – Chiang Mai, Thailand

Well it's official, I made it through the twenty-six-day Vipassana meditation course. It was an experience that had good days and not so good days, but I am so happy I did it. Just making it to the end is an accomplishment for me. Many people came and went, as it was a struggle to even make it to the tenth day. We practiced to be mindful and aware of everything we were doing. Sitting, walking, eating, drinking, seeing, hearing, and as my mind began to slow down, so did my world.

Morning bells rang at 4 a.m. and one of the bells was right outside my room, which a nun would ring literally almost a hundred times, and these bells were LOUD. Then we'd meditate until the breakfast bell went at 6:30 a.m., have breakfast, meditate some more, then the lunch bell would go at 10:30 a.m. Before each meal we had to wait for everyone to be seated, then we'd wait for the chanting and prayers to begin. Lunch was the last meal of the day, as there was no food allowed after noon. Only liquids permitted afterward, so I drank tons and tons of water and hot water with honey.

There were days I felt completely wiped and exhausted, especially when the temperature was 38 degrees Celsius, about 104 degrees Fahrenheit! I literally avoided being in the sun ninety-nine percent of the time, spending my time in the mediation hall or my room with fans on the wall. But one of my most favorite things to do was drink water in the shade on a log stool, listening to the monks chanting in the main temple in the afternoons after a practice. In these moments, nothing else mattered, just being in the moment was all there was, and I felt an incredible feeling of calmness and contentment. When my cup was empty, I'd fill it again, and again and again and again…mindfully "drinking, drinking, drinking." After meditating for hours on end each day, I have come to know myself so much more than knew before. I learned what I like, what I don't like, what makes me happy, what makes me sad, and what triggers me. Many things came up from the past to be healed and released. There was a lot of forgiveness and letting go, which is easier said than done.

I became aware of my true values and took action for what I felt was right and not right. For example, it was a routine to scrape our food waste after each meal into garbage cans. Around the seventh or eighth day, after scraping half a tray of food into the garbage, I thought, "Why am I doing this? I don't waste food, ever, and now I'm contributing to garbage bins that are reaching the top with leftovers." I thought of the people in Nepal, who are struggling every day to get food on their table, and here we are carelessly throwing it away. I got so emotional and after that day, I never joined the line to empty my tray again. I asked the kitchen for only fruits, and I bought salads from the store on site. It felt so good to be eating healthy food while not getting over served or overeating.

Then there were moments of overwhelming emotions of gratefulness of the simplest things we take for granted—clean water being one of them. Having cold showers felt like a blessing. At times I didn't want to meditate at all, and I learned to just be kind, gentle, and compassionate toward myself. The mind causes a lot of suffering for us, and sometimes we don't even realize it. Meditation helps you pinpoint and observe your thinking patterns, and you'll learn things about yourself you never knew before!

Being mindful and aware of everything you do is so important in your everyday life. Please know that everything you do, say, hear, feel, and every action and conversation you have with someone is stored in your memory. The mind will pull up these random memories and replay them in your thoughts for days, months, and even years later. If someone treats you badly, or did something to you that you didn't like, this may come up over and over, affecting your state of well-being. As soon as you realize things from the past still hurt you, that is a sign forgiveness is needed. Sending love, compassion, and kindness to that person and yourself will set you free. And think of the people you may have hurt out of resentment, anger, jealousy, or maybe not intentionally. These actions may affect the receiver for days, months, or years as well, replaying your actions in their minds. It can be a vicious cycle. So choose to be kind, loving, compassionate toward everyone you meet, your friends, your family. No one's perfect, but you can learn to be more mindful.

The last four days and three nights, I spent locked alone in my room, a thing called "Determination." Direction given was to meditate one hour walking, one hour sitting, then one hour walking, one hour sitting, with some breaks in between, without sleeping. This was something I had no interest in doing, but I did my best anyway. Food would be delivered to my room in a bag and placed on my door. On the second day of Determination, my lunch was delivered at 10 a.m. It was a packaged veggie salad and a bag of lychees, a sweet, popular Thai fruit. I got the salad ready in my steel bowl, cut up an apple, and threw it in, then mixed the dressing. The bell went at 10:30 a.m., and I patiently waited for the prayers to begin. Thinking that maybe I maybe missed the prayers, as I could just seldom hear them in the kitchen area from my room, and it was going on 11 a.m. I decided okay, I've patiently waited for an hour; they should have said the prayers by now, I think I will just eat. As soon as I had my first bites of lettuce on my fork, the familiar sounds of the nun's voice began to speak on the microphone. I immediately put my fork down, bowed three times and put my hands in prayer. Grateful I didn't take that first bite as I listened to the Thai chants, which was like music to my ears. Never ever in my life have I waited over an hour to eat food that was sitting right in front of me. That was a true test of patience and willpower. Again, the people of Nepal crossed my mind and what it's like to be hungry.

After completion of the course, I spent the day with other meditators from around the world—Poland, Australia, United States... We shared our experiences and said things that only meditators would understand. Like kissing the shower-head after a shower. Yes, that happened...I had a moment LOL. Meditation puts you in a state of such gratitude that you appreciate things you wouldn't normally, where tears of joy just fall down your face as your heart bursts open.

When we left the center, we went to the old city. We decided to get food at noon and walked around to find a good restaurant. Cars honked at us when we crossed street because we were going so slow, and it didn't even faze us. I just kept walking with a knowing of "crossing the street, the light has turned, cars are honking, it's all good" and we got to the other side. We found ourselves meditating in front of huge Buddha statues in temples and would say, "Let's go get food," and we would leave. Four and a half hours later, we enjoyed delicious Thai dishes and coconut milkshakes. Only God knows where the time went.

I have been teaching meditation to people I meet along my travels and to groups who would come to the last meditation center where I was staying. What I liked about the twenty-six-day course is that it has given me new techniques and a solid foundation to the practice.

If anyone is interested in learning more about meditation or has any questions or experiences you'd like to share with me, let me know. If you're one of those people who doesn't even know where to start, I'll get you started. I am going to start to teach over Skype, so if you'd like to have a session or a chat, just send me a message.

There are many more things that are definitely worth sharing, but that would turn into a Facebook book. So I'll leave it at that for now. Thanks for all the encouragement I had going into it, for all of the messages of "thinking about you" and "sending love" I've received while I was gone. And thanks to Tim, who encouraged me to do the twenty-six days when I had only planned on doing ten, and thank you to everyone who has supported my karma trip and to those who have helped me out along the way!

Last but not least, I highly recommend the ten-day Vipassana course. It's offered all over the world, and courses run all year long and will change your life for the better.

Now that I am out in the real world in Chiang Mai, I am in a state of bliss. All I want to do is be in peace and solitude, gazing at the luscious green courtyard of my hostel with waterfalls, roosters, and butterflies, with a good possibility of a dance party to music that rocks my ears. Thanks for reading!

Blessings and be kind,

Amanda XoXo ♥

And that is that.

Falling Mangoes.

Thanks for reading!

I encourage each and every one of you to take the time to learn how to meditate and incorporate it into your daily lives. There are silent meditation centers around the world that are free or by donation. I highly recommend doing the common Vipassana ten-day retreat, and if you do it, I guarantee that you will experience more peace in your life.

Inner peace = Outer peace.

Do it for you and do it for the world. Namaste.

P.S. After the retreat, I flew to Los Angeles just in time to celebrate His Holiness the Dalai Lama's eightieth on July 6, 2015. It was such an honor to be in his presence on this special day, to see his smile, and to receive a blessing from him within moments of him coming out on to the stage. These are things I'll remember forever. He is one of the greatest symbols of peace for our world, and I am so fortunate to have connected with him in four countries in the last four years. This book is dedicated to him too.

Thank you, Dalai Lama, for your lifelong work, your compassion, and your love. You will forever remain in the hearts of those touched by your presence and way of being. You inspire me more than you'll ever know. I love you.

Amanda (Or as you would say…"Canada") ♥

www.ingramcontent.com/pod-product-compliance
Lightning Source LLC
Chambersburg PA
CBHW051927220626
47052CB00003B/613